# Snippets of Marilyn Monroe

DAVE FARNHAM

# DISCLAIMER

While every effort has been made to ensure the
information in this book is correct, human error is
always a possibility and therefore the author cannot
accept responsibility for any inaccuracies.

.

# CONTENTS

# INTRODUCTION

In a game of Word Association, if anyone says 'Dumb Blonde', you can be almost certain that the words 'Marilyn Monroe' will follow. This shows a public perception that has endured since her untimely death in 1962.

Born Norma Jean Mortenson (later Baker), Marilyn was actually far from 'dumb' as anyone reading her biography will know (and actually, she was not a natural blonde, either, so both words are misfits – which, coincidentally was the title of her last film). Her mother was unstable and unable to look after Norma Jean, whose formative years were restless as she was moved from one place to another, including an orphanage, aunts' homes and a friend's house (where she later claimed to have been sexually abused).

It is no surprise, given her background, that she spent much of her all-too-brief adult life seeking stability and love, being married and seeking divorces three times, nor that she loved the public adoration that came her way in the way a child loves to be noticed. Hers was an unhappy and ultimately unfulfilled life in spite of the fame and wealth she enjoyed.

That she was an intelligent, many-faceted personality becomes evident from the fascinating collection of quotes to be found in this book. Read them and then reflect again on the epithet 'Dumb Blonde'...

# BIO

Marilyn Monroe

Real name Norma Jeane Mortenson

**1926** June 1ˢᵗ Born in Los Angeles. Mother was Gladys Pearl Baker, a film-cutter at a movie studio and recently separated from her second husband Martin Mortensen. Norma's surname according to her birth certificate was Mortenson (note the different spelling) but Gladys had the child's surname changed to Baker, that of her first husband. At twelve days old, the infant Norma was fostered by a deeply religious couple, Ida and Wayne Bolender. Her mother visited her every Saturday.

**1933** Moved back in with her mother, who had become mentally unstable.

**1935** Gladys broke down completely and was admitted to a mental hospital. Norma Jeane was placed in the care of an orphanage.

**1937**  Her mother's best friend, Grace McKee, who had just married Ervin 'Doc' Goddard, took her in to live with them.  Norma later claimed that Ervin sexually abused her.  She left the Goddards' home and went to live first with one aunt, then another.

**1942**  Moved back in with the Goddards.  Met her first serious boyfriend, James Dougherty and married him that year.

**1943**  James joined the Merchant Marine and was sent to the Pacific.  Whilst he was away, Norma took a job in a munitions factory, where a photographer, taking photos to boost morale in the war effort, spotted her and suggested she try modelling.  She joined the Blue Book Modelling Agency and dyed her hair blonde to meet their requirements.  She was instantly successful, appearing on magazine covers. She was noticed by Ben Lyon of Twentieth Century Fox studios (and later star of the 1950s sitcom '*Life With The Lyons*'), who signed her on a six-month contract.  He felt she needed a name change and suggested Marilyn.  She added to it her mother's maiden surname, Monroe.

**1946**  She divorced James Dougherty.  Appeared in a few minor film roles.

**1947**  Performed in *Dangerous Years*, the first film in which her name appeared on the credits.  She then left Twentieth Century Fox.

**1948**  Met agent Johnny Hyde and joined Columbia Pictures.  Gained her first major role in *Ladies Of The Chorus*.

**1949**  Dropped by Columbia.  Posed for a series of nude photographs.  Had a minor role in Marx Brothers film *Love Happy*.

**1950**  Had several minor film roles then gained a much bigger part in MGM film *The Asphalt Jungle*, a successful appearance, as was her next role in *All About Eve*.  She signed a seven-year contract with Twentieth Century Fox.

**1951**  She enrolled for a course in Art Appreciation and Literature at Univerity of California (UCAL), whilst continuing her film career in a series of low-budget and unremarkable films.

**1952**  Some of her nude photos appeared on calendars.  The press wanted to know the identity of the model in the photos and Marilyn confessed that is was her, explaining she had posed only because she needed to pay her bills.  This gained her public sympathy.  One of the pictures was reproduced in *Playboy* Magazine, boosting the magazine's circulation and making Marilyn famous; she was featured on the cover of *Life* Magazine.  More film roles followed including *Monkey Business* and *Niagra*, during which she started to exhibit signs of stage fright.  She started dating baseball star Joe DiMaggio.

**1953**  Starred alongside Jane Russell in *Gentlemen Prefer Blondes*, in which she sang 'Diamonds Are A Girl's Best Friend'.  The film was very successful.

**1954**  Married Joe DiMaggio in January.  They divorced in November of that year.  During that time she appeared in several popular films, including *The Seven Year Itch*.

**1955**   She started dating playwright Arthur Miller (author of *Death of a Salesman* and The *Crucible*).   At the same time she was taking acting lessons in an attempt to overcome her stage fright.

**1956**   A very successful appearance in *Bus Stop*.   She married Arthur Miller on June 29th and converted to Judaism.

**1957**   A major starring role in *The Prince And The Showgirl*, directed by Sir Lawrence Olivier, gained her several nominations and awards.   Monroe suffered a miscarriage in August.

**1958**   Starred in *Some Like It Hot* to great critical acclaim, though during filming her behaviour became difficult and unpredictable.   She won the Golden Globe Award for her performance.   Suffered another miscarriage in December.

**1959**   Acted in *Let's Make Love*, alongside Yves Montand, with whom she had a brief affair.   The film was considered a disappointment.   At the same time, her health began to suffer; she experienced insomnia and became increasingly reliant on prescribed medication. She began seeing a psychiatrist.

**1960** Miller wrote the screenplay for *The Misfits*, which was the last complete film Monroe acted in, alongside Clark Gable among others.   It was filmed in the Nevada Desert.   Monroe became increasingly dependent on alcohol and sleeping pills and spent ten days in hospital during the film's shooting.   Although the film was not a success at the time, critics now regard it as her greatest performance. Clark Gable died of a heart attack soon after the filming ended.   Monroe announced her separation from Arthur Miller.

**1961**    Granted divorce from Miller in January.    In February she entered a psychiatric clinic, followed by a period in hospital undergoing surgery.

**1962**  Bought her first (and only) house, in Los Angeles. In May, she attended President Kennedy's birthday party and famously sang Happy Birthday to him. (This was filmed and the video can be seen on YouTube).  Started filming *Something's Got To Give* but failed to turn up so often that she was sacked and the film remained uncompleted.  (It was later remade with a new cast including Doris Day, under the title *Move Over Darling*).

On August 5th she was found dead in the bedroom of her house.  An autopsy revealed barbiturate poisoning and 'possible suicide' but conspiracy theories still abound, many believing she was murdered.  No evidence for this has ever been found.

# ABOUT HERSELF

"What good is it being Marilyn Monroe? Why can't I just be an ordinary woman?"

*

"I restore myself when I'm alone."

*

"I'm selfish, impatient, and a little insecure. I make mistakes, I'm out of control, and at times hard to handle. But if you can't handle me at my worst, then you sure as hell don't deserve me at my best."

*

"Sometimes I've been to a party where no one spoke to me for a whole evening. The men, frightened by their wives or sweeties, would give me a wide berth. And the ladies would gang up in a corner to discuss my dangerous character."

\*

"The 'public' scares me, but people I trust."

\*

"I want to grow old without facelifts. I want to have the courage to be loyal to the face I have made."

\*

"I once wanted to prove myself by being a great actress. Now I want to prove that I'm a person. Then maybe I'll be a great actress."

\*

"I was brought up differently than the average American child because the average child is brought up expecting to be happy."

\*

"I don't want everybody to see exactly where I live, what my sofa or my fireplace looks like."

\*

"I have always had a talent for irritating women since I was fourteen."

\*

"The nicest thing for me is sleep, then at least I can dream."

\*

"I am not a victim of emotional conflicts. I am human."

\*

"I've never fooled anyone. I've let people fool themselves. They didn't bother to find out who and what I was. Instead they would invent a character for me. I wouldn't argue with them. They were obviously loving somebody I wasn't."

*

"I am alone; I am always alone no matter what."

*

"I have been told my eating habits are absolutely bizarre. But I don't think so."

*

"If I'd observed all the rules, I'd never have got anywhere."

*

"The thing I want more than anything else? I want to have children. I used to feel for every child I had, I would adopt another."

*

"I am trying to find myself. Sometimes that's not easy."

*

"I'm very definitely a woman and I enjoy it."

*

"I often wake up in the night, and I like to have something to think about."

*

"I am invariably late for appointments - sometimes as much as two hours. I've tried to change my ways but the things that make me late are too strong, and too pleasing."

*

"When I was 11, the whole world was closed to me. I just felt I was on the outside of the world."

*

"No one ever told me I was pretty when I was a little girl. All little girls should be told they're pretty, even if they aren't."

*

"I've never dropped anyone I believed in."

*

"I read poetry to save time."

*

"When Clark Gable died, I cried for 2 days straight. I couldn't eat or sleep."

*

"I don't look at myself as a commodity, but I'm sure a lot of people have."

*

"What do I wear in bed? Why, Chanel No. 5, of course."

*

"I used to get the feeling, and sometimes I still get it, that I was fooling somebody - I don't know who or what - maybe myself. I have feelings some days where there are scenes with a lot of responsibility, and I'll wish, 'Gee, if only I had been a cleaning woman.'"

*

"It's not true I had nothing on, I had the radio on."

*

"Someone said to me, 'If fifty percent of the experts in Hollywood said you had no talent and should give up, what would you do?' My answer was then and still is, 'If a hundred percent told me that, all one hundred percent would be wrong.'"

*

"At twelve I looked like a girl of seventeen. My body was developed and shapely. I still wore the blue dress and the blouse the orphanage provided. They made me look like an overgrown lummox."

*

"I learned to walk as a baby, and I haven't had a lesson since."

\*

"I just got to feel that whoever I marry has some real regard for me."

\*

"Having a child, that's always been my biggest fear. I want a child and I fear a child."

\*

"If there is only one thing in my life that I am proud of, it's that I've never been a kept woman."

\*

"For a long time I was scared I'd find out I was like my mother."

\*

"I don't digest things with my mind."

*

"I am good, but not an angel. I do sin, but I am not the devil. I am just a small girl in a big world trying to find someone to love."

*

"It's better to be unhappy alone than unhappy with someone - so far."

*

"I like to feel blonde all over."

*

"I never wanted to be Marilyn - it just happened. Marilyn's like a veil I wear over Norma Jeane."

*

"I've always wanted a baby."

*

"I have too many fantasies to be a housewife. I guess I am a fantasy."

*

"I don't want to make money, I just want to be wonderful."

*

"I don't mind living in a man's world as long as I can be a woman in it."

*

"I'm one of the world's most self-conscious people. I really have to struggle."

*

"Like any creative human being, I would like a bit more control so that it would be a little easier for me when the director says, 'One tear, right now,' that one tear would pop out."

\*

"My work is the only ground I've ever had to stand on. I seem to have a whole superstructure with no foundation but I'm working on the foundation."

\*

"All my stepchildren carried the burden of my fame. Sometimes they would read terrible things about me, and I'd worry about whether it would hurt them. I would tell them: 'Don't hide these things from me. I'd rather you ask me these things straight out, and I'll answer all your questions.'"

\*

"I wish I knew why I am so anguished."

\*

"Someday I want to have children and give them all the love I never had."

\*

"Dogs never bite me - just humans."

\*

"I don't consider myself an intellectual. And this is not one of my aims. But I admire intellectual people."

\*

"I don't mind making jokes, but I don't want to look like one."

\*

"Some of my foster families used to send me to the movies to get me out of the house and there I'd sit all day and way into the night. Up in front, there with the screen so big, a little kid all alone, and I loved it. I loved anything that moved up there and I didn't miss anything that happened and there was no popcorn either."

\*

"I think I have always had a little humor."

\*

"Sometimes I feel my whole life has been one big rejection."

*

"Of course, it does depend on the people, but sometimes I'm invited places to kind of brighten up a dinner table like a musician who'll play the piano after dinner, and I know you're not really invited for yourself. You're just an ornament."

*

"I defy gravity."

*

"I knew I belonged to the public and to the world, not because I was talented or even beautiful, but because I had never belonged to anything or anyone else."

*

"I know I will never be happy, but I know I can be gay!"

*

"I've been on a calendar, but I've never been on time."

*

"It's often just enough to be with someone. I don't need to touch them. Not even talk. A feeling passes between you both. You're not alone."

*

"I love a natural look in pictures."

*

"What good am I? I can't have kids. I can't cook. I've been divorced three times. Who would want me?"

*

"You know, most people really don't know me."

*

"When it comes down to it, I let them think what they want. If they care enough to bother with what I do, then I'm already better than them."

\*

"I have feelings too. I am still human. All I want is to be loved, for myself and for my talent."

\*

"Beneath the makeup and behind the smile I am just a girl who wishes for the world."

\*

"If I'd observed all the rules I'd never have got anywhere."

\*

"If I play a stupid girl and ask a stupid question, I've got to follow it through, what am I supposed to do, look intelligent?"

\*

"Some people have been unkind. If I say I want to grow as an actress, they look at my figure. If I say I want to develop, to learn my craft, they laugh. Somehow they don't expect me to be serious about my work."

# ABOUT LIFE

"We should all start to live before we get too old. Fear is stupid. So are regrets."

\*

"I believe that everything happens for a reason. People change so that you can learn to let go, things go wrong so that you appreciate them when they're right, you believe lies so you eventually learn to trust no one but yourself, and sometimes good things fall apart so better things can fall together."

\*

"This life is what you make it. No matter what, you're going to mess up sometimes, it's a universal truth. But the good part is you get to decide how you're going to mess it up. Girls will be your friends - they'll act like it anyway. But just remember, some come, some go. The ones that stay with you through everything - they're your true best friends. Don't let go of them. Also remember, sisters make the best friends in the world. As for lovers, well, they'll come and go too. And baby, I hate to say it, most of them - actually pretty much all of them are going to break your heart, but you can't give up because if you give up, you'll never find your soulmate. You'll never find that half who makes you whole and that goes for everything. Just because you fail once, doesn't mean you're gonna fail at everything. Keep trying, hold on, and always, always, always believe in yourself, because if you don't, then who will, sweetie? So keep your head high, keep your chin up, and most importantly, keep smiling, because life's a beautiful thing and there's so much to smile about."

\*

"Ever notice how 'What the hell' is always the right answer?"

\*

"A wise girl kisses but doesn't love, listens but doesn't believe, and leaves before she is left."

\*

"I am involved in a freedom ride protesting the loss of the minority rights belonging to the few remaining earthbound stars. All we demanded was our right to twinkle."

\*

"Nothing's ever easy as long as you go on living."

\*

"It's not too much fun to know yourself too well or think you do - everyone needs a little conceit to carry them through and past the falls."

\*

"Respect is one of life's greatest treasures. I mean, what does it all add up to if you don't have that?"

\*

"We should all start to live before we get too old."

\*

"Imperfection is beauty, madness is genius and it's better to be absolutely ridiculous than absolutely boring."

*

"A career is born in public - talent in privacy."

*

"We human beings are strange creatures and still reserve the right to think for ourselves."

*

"A career is wonderful, but you can't curl up with it on a cold night."

*

"Sometimes I think it would be easier to avoid old age, to die young, but then you'd never complete your life, would you? You'd never wholly know you."

*

"The public doesn't mind people living together without being married, providing they don't overdo it."

*

"Millions of people live their entire lives without finding themselves. But it is something I must do."

*

"It's all make believe, isn't it?"

*

"If you spend your life competing with business men, what do you have? A bank account and ulcers!"

*

"Creativity has got to start with humanity and when you're a human being, you feel, you suffer. You're gay, you're sick, you're nervous or whatever."

*

"Who said nights were for sleep?"

\*

"Wanting to be someone else is a waste of the person you are."

\*

Love and work are the only two real things in our lives. They belong together, otherwise it is off. Work is in itself a form of love."

\*

"When you're young and healthy you can plan on Monday to commit suicide, and by Wednesday you're laughing again."

# ABOUT ACTING AND FAME

"I've always felt toward the slightest scene, even if all I had to do in a scene was just to come in and say, 'Hi,' that the people ought to get their money's worth and that this is an obligation of mine, to give them the best you can get from me."

\*

"I myself would like to become more disciplined within my work."

\*

"If a star or studio chief or any other great movie personages find themselves sitting among a lot of nobodies, they get frightened - as if somebody was trying to demote them."

*

"I don't know if high society is different in other cities, but in Hollywood, important people can't stand to be invited someplace that isn't full of other important people. They don't mind a few unfamous people being present because they make good listeners."

*

"I've often stood silent at a party for hours listening to my movie idols turn into dull and little people."

*

"Success makes so many people hate you. I wish it wasn't that way. It would be wonderful to enjoy success without seeing envy in the eyes of those around you."

*

"I enjoy acting when you really hit it right."

*

"Dreaming about being an actress, is more exciting then being one."

*

"I used to think as I looked out on the Hollywood night, 'There must be thousands of girls sitting alone like me dreaming of being a movie star.' But I'm not going to worry about them. I'm dreaming the hardest."

*

"Fame is fickle, and I know it. It has its compensations but it also has its drawbacks, and I've experienced them both."

*

"I want to be an artist, an actress with integrity, and that includes all kinds of parts."

*

"An actor is supposed to be a sensitive instrument."

*

"There is a need for aloneness, which I don't think most people realise for an actor. It's almost having certain kinds of secrets for yourself that you'll let the whole world in on only for a moment, when you're acting. But everybody is always tugging at you. They'd all like sort of a chunk of you."

\*

"I like actors very much, but to marry one would be like marrying your brother. You look too much alike in the mirror."

\*

"I want to be an artist, not... a celluloid aphrodisiac."

\*

"Hollywood is a place where they'll pay you a thousand dollars for a kiss and fifty cents for your soul."

\*

"Only the public can make a star. It's the studios who try to make a system out of it."

\*

"An actress is not a machine, but they treat you like a machine. A money machine."

\*

"Fame will go by and, so long, I've had you, fame. If it goes by, I've always known it was fickle. So at least it's something I experience, but that's not where I live."

\*

"There was my name up in lights. I said, 'God, somebody's made a mistake.' But there it was, in lights. And I sat there and said, 'Remember, you're not a star.' Yet there it was up in lights."

\*

"If I'm a star, then the people made me a star."

\*

"Fame is like caviar, you know - it's good to have caviar

but not when you have it at every meal."

*

"I think that when you are famous every weakness is exaggerated."

*

"We are all of us stars, and we deserve to twinkle."

*

"I'm looking forward to becoming a marvelous - excuse the word marvelous - character actress. like Marie Dressler, like Will Rogers."

*

"An actor is supposed to be a sensitive instrument. Isaac Stern takes good care of his violin. What if everybody jumped on his violin?"

*

"Fame doesn't fulfill you. It warms you a bit, but that

warmth is temporary."

*

"With fame, you know, you can read about yourself, somebody else's ideas about you, but what's important is how you feel about yourself - for survival and living day to day with what comes up."

*

"When I was five I think, that's when I started wanting to be an actress."

*

"I live to succeed, not to please you or anyone else."

*

"I love to do the things the censors won't pass."

*

"Looking back, I guess I used to play-act all the time. For one thing, it meant I could live in a more interesting world than the one around me."

*

"If I close my eyes and think of Hollywood, all I see is one big varicose vein."

*

"I'm for the individual as opposed to the corporation. The way it is the individual is the underdog, and with all the things a corporation has going for them the individual comes out banged on her head. The artist is nothing. It's really tragic. "

# ABOUT CLOTHES AND GOOD LOOKS

"Why is it you always meet people when you look your worst?"

*

"There isn't anybody that looks like me without clothes on."

*

"Designers want me to dress like Spring, in billowing things. I don't feel like Spring. I feel like a warm red Autumn."

*

"Beauty and femininity are ageless and can't be contrived, and glamour, although the manufacturers won't like this, cannot be manufactured. Not real glamour; it's based on femininity."

*

"The body is meant to be seen, not all covered up."

*

"I want the world to see my body."

*

"I always have a full-length mirror next to the camera when I'm doing publicity stills. That way, I know how I look."

*

"In Hollywood a girl's virtue is much less important than her hairdo."

*

"I don't know who invented high heels, but all women owe him a lot."

\*

"I won't be satisfied until people want to hear me sing without looking at me. Of course, that doesn't mean I want them to stop looking."

\*

" If you're gonna be two-faced at least make one of them pretty."

\*

"To all the girls that think you're fat because you're not a size zero, you're the beautiful one, its society who's ugly."

\*

"Your clothes should be tight enough to show you're a woman but loose enough to show you're a lady"

# ABOUT FRIENDSHIP

"Friends accept you the way you are."

*

"Experts on romance say for a happy marriage there has to be more than a passionate love. For a lasting union, they insist, there must be a genuine liking for each other. Which, in my book, is a good definition for friendship."

*

"I'll think I have a few wonderful friends and all of a sudden, ooh, here it comes. They do a lot of things. They talk about you to the press, to their friends, tell stories, and you know, it's disappointing."

*

"I remember when I was in high school I didn't have a new dress for each special occasion. The girls would bring the fact to my attention, not always too delicately. The boys, however, never bothered with the subject. They were my friends, not because of the size of my wardrobe but because they liked me."

*

"What I really want to say: That what the world really needs is a real feeling of kinship. Everybody: stars, laborers, Negroes, Jews, Arabs. We are all brothers."

*

"I think one of the basic reasons men make good friends is that they can make up their minds quickly."

*

"Friendship is the bestiest thing that comes to life. Friends will always be there for you don't worry about the fakes worry about the people who had your back from the start and never treated you wrong always remember they are your real friends don't never take them as granted because one day your going to lose a good friend by the way your action's are when you see a good friend stick to that person."

*

"When you have a good friend that really cares for you and tries to stick in there with you, you treat them like nothing. Learn to be a good friend because one day you're gonna look up and say I lost a good friend. Learn how to be respectful to your friends, don't just start arguments with them and don't tell them the reason, always remember your friends will be there quicker than your family. Learn to remember you got great friends, don't forget that and they will always care for you no matter what. Always remember to smile and look up at what you got in life."

# ABOUT MEN, LOVE AND SEX

"Sex is a part of nature. I go along with nature."

\*

"The working men, I'll go by and they'll whistle. At first they whistle because they think, 'Oh, it's a girl. She's got blond hair and she's not out of shape,' and then they say, 'Gosh, it's Marilyn Monroe!'"

\*

"The trouble with censors is that they worry if a girl has cleavage. They ought to worry if she hasn't any."

\*

"How do I know about a man's needs for a sex symbol? I'm a girl."

\*

"In fact, my popularity seems almost entirely a masculine phenomenon."

\*

"A man has a tendency to accept you the way you are, while most women immediately start to pick flaws and want to change you."

\*

"Men who think that a woman's past love affairs lessen her love for them are usually stupid and weak."

\*

"The fact is that I find more most men are more open, more generous, and much more stimulating than the majority of females I know."

*

"The real lover is the man who can thrill you just by touching your head or smiling into your eyes - or just by staring into space."

*

"Arthur Miller wouldn't have married me if I had been nothing but a dumb blonde."

*

"Men are so willing to respect anything that bores them."

*

"When I was a youngster I lived with different families. I nearly always felt closer to the man of the house. Maybe because I always dreamed of having a father of my own."

*

"My public is growing up just as I am. After all, I'm not 19 anymore and if I stick with the sex bit, who will be paying to see me when I'm 50?"

*

"I think that sexuality is only attractive when it's natural and spontaneous."

*

"We are all born sexual creatures,thank God, but it's a pity so many people despise and crush this natural gift."

*

"I've found men are less likely to let petty things annoy them."

*

"I guess I have always been deeply terrified to really be someone's wife since I know from life one cannot love another, ever, really."

*

"Being a sex symbol is a heavy load to carry, especially when one is tired, hurt and bewildered."

*

"There is just no comparison between having a dinner date with a man and staying home playing canasta with the girls."

*

"A strong man doesn't have to be dominant toward a woman. He doesn't match his strength against a woman weak with love for him. He matches it against the world."

*

"A man is more frank and sincere with his emotions than a woman. We girls, I'm afraid, have a tendency to hide our feelings."

*

"Marriage destroyed my relationship with two wonderful men."

*

"Confidentially, the type of male I find most enjoyable for a friend is one who has enough fire and assurance to speak up for his convictions."

\*

"When it comes to gossip, I have to readily admit men are as guilty as women."

\*

"Consider the fellow. He never spends his time telling you about his previous night's date. You get the idea he has eyes only for you and wouldn't think of looking at another woman."

\*

"Husbands are chiefly good as lovers when they are betraying their wives."

\*

"Naturally, there are times when every woman likes to be flattered... to feel she is the most important thing in someone's world. Only a man can paint this picture."

*

"I have noticed... that men usually leave married women alone and are inclined to treat all wives with respect. This is no great credit to married women."

*

"If your man is a sports enthusiast, you may have to resign yourself to his spouting off in a monotone on a prize fight, football game or pennant race."

*

"Before marriage, a girl has to make love to a man to hold him. After marriage, she has to hold him to make love to him."

*

"Next to my husband, and along with Marlon Brando, I think that Yves Montand is the most attractive man I've ever met."

*

"A sex symbol becomes a thing. I just hate to be a thing."

\*

"It is wonderful to have someone praise you, to be desired."

\*

"Girdles and wire stays should have never been invented. No man wants to hug a padded bird cage."

\*

"I could never pretend something I didn't feel. I could never make love if I didn't love, and if I loved I could no more hide the fact than change the color of my eyes."

\*

"Most men judge your importance in their lives by how much you can hurt them."

# HER VIEW OF WOMANHOOD

"A woman knows by intuition, or instinct, what is best for herself."

*

"Black men don't like to be called 'boys,' but women accept being called 'girls.'"

*

"A smart girl leaves before she is left."

*

"If you can make a girl laugh, you can make her do anything."

\*

"A man makes you feel important - makes you glad you are a woman."

\*

"One of the best things that ever happened to me is that I'm a woman. That is the way all females should feel."

\*

"Give a girl the right shoes, and she can conquer the world."

\*

"There are many times when a woman will ask another girl friend how she likes her new hat. She will reply, 'Fine,' but slap her hand to her forehead the minute the girl leaves to yipe, 'What a horror!'"

\*

"A woman can't be alone. She needs a man. A man and a woman support and strengthen each other. She just can't do it by herself."

*

"Girls shouldn't worry about being the equal of men in the business world."

*

"A woman can bring a new love to each man she loves, providing there are not too many."

*

"Women who seek to be equal with men lack ambition."

*

"How wrong it is for a woman to expect the man to build the world she wants, rather than to create it herself."

*

"A girl doesn't need anyone who doesn't need her"

*

"A wise girl knows her limits, a smart girl knows that she has none."

DAVE FARNHAM

# OTHER BOOKS BY DAVE FARNHAM

Snippets of Richard Attenborough

Snippets of Billy Connolly

Snippets of Paul Gascoigne

Snippets of Jeremy Kyle

Snippets of Boris Johnson

Snippets of Nigel Farage

Snippets of Joan Rivers

Gandhi's Teachings for Troubled Times

Snippets of Oscar Wilde